WHAT IS WATER?

CONTENTS

SCIENCE ALIVE

WHAT IS WATER?

Pure water has no colour, taste, or smell. Yet it is one of the most important substances on earth. The bodies of all living things are composed mostly of water. Without water, life would be either impossible or very different from what we know.

Water comes in many different forms. It can be snow, frost, ice, fog, mist, hail, or steam. Water is the only abundant substance that changes between the *gas*, *liquid*, and *solid* states within the normal range of temperatures on earth. These changes are necessary for life. For example, if water was unable to change from a gas to a liquid, there would be no rain.

Over 70 per cent of the earth's surface is water. There are about 1.4 billion cubic kilometres of water on the planet.

H$_2$O STANDS FOR WATER

Scientists use the symbol H$_2$O to stand for water. It means that a molecule of water is made up of two hydrogen atoms joined to one oxygen atom. No matter what form water takes, it's always made up of water molecules. A single drop of water can contain billions of molecules.

The molecules in solids vibrate. When ice melts to become a liquid, the molecules vibrate faster and become free to move about. These movements are far too fast and too small for people to see. The molecules move even more vigorously when the water warms. As the water boils, they escape from the liquid to form a gas in the air.

In 1805, the French scientist Joseph-Louis Gay-Lussac and the German scientist Alexander von Humboldt made an important discovery. Their experiments showed that water contains two volumes of hydrogen for every one volume of oxygen.

DIAGRAM OF A WATER MOLECULE

One water molecule is made up of three atoms. Two hydrogen atoms are linked to one oxygen atom.

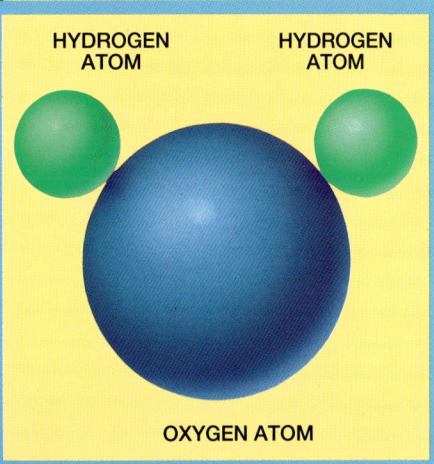

HYDROGEN ATOM

HYDROGEN ATOM

OXYGEN ATOM

WATER AS A LIQUID

We are most familiar with water in its liquid form. Water is usually a liquid between the temperatures of 0°C and 100°C. It can *dissolve* more substances than any other common liquid, and forms the basis of a wide variety of water-based substances, including plant sap, fruit juice, and toothpaste.

The molecules in liquid water are held together by weak attractive forces. This means that although the molecules usually stay together in drops or larger pools, they can flow over each other easily, or break up into smaller droplets.

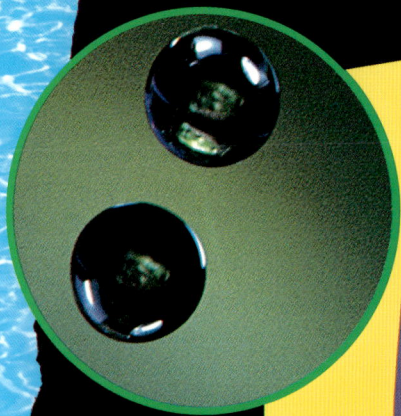

Most of the liquids we drink, such as milk and fruit juice, are simply various substances dissolved in water.

Some plants, such as aloe vera, are so full of water that the sap drips out when a leaf or stem is snapped.

7

WATER AS A GAS

The hotter liquid water gets, the faster its molecules vibrate and move about, and the weaker the attraction between the molecules becomes. Eventually, the molecules with the highest energy can escape from the liquid to become a colourless gas in the air. When this happens slowly, it is called *evaporation*. Only a few molecules have enough energy to break away, or evaporate, at any time.

When water reaches 100°C, it boils and becomes *steam*. Millions of water molecules vibrate very fast, pushing each other apart with great force. Some power stations use steam to turn huge turbines that produce electricity. Steam is an invisible gas. It sometimes cools to form a mist of liquid water, which we can see.

Geothermal power stations harness the energy from underground steam to produce electricity.

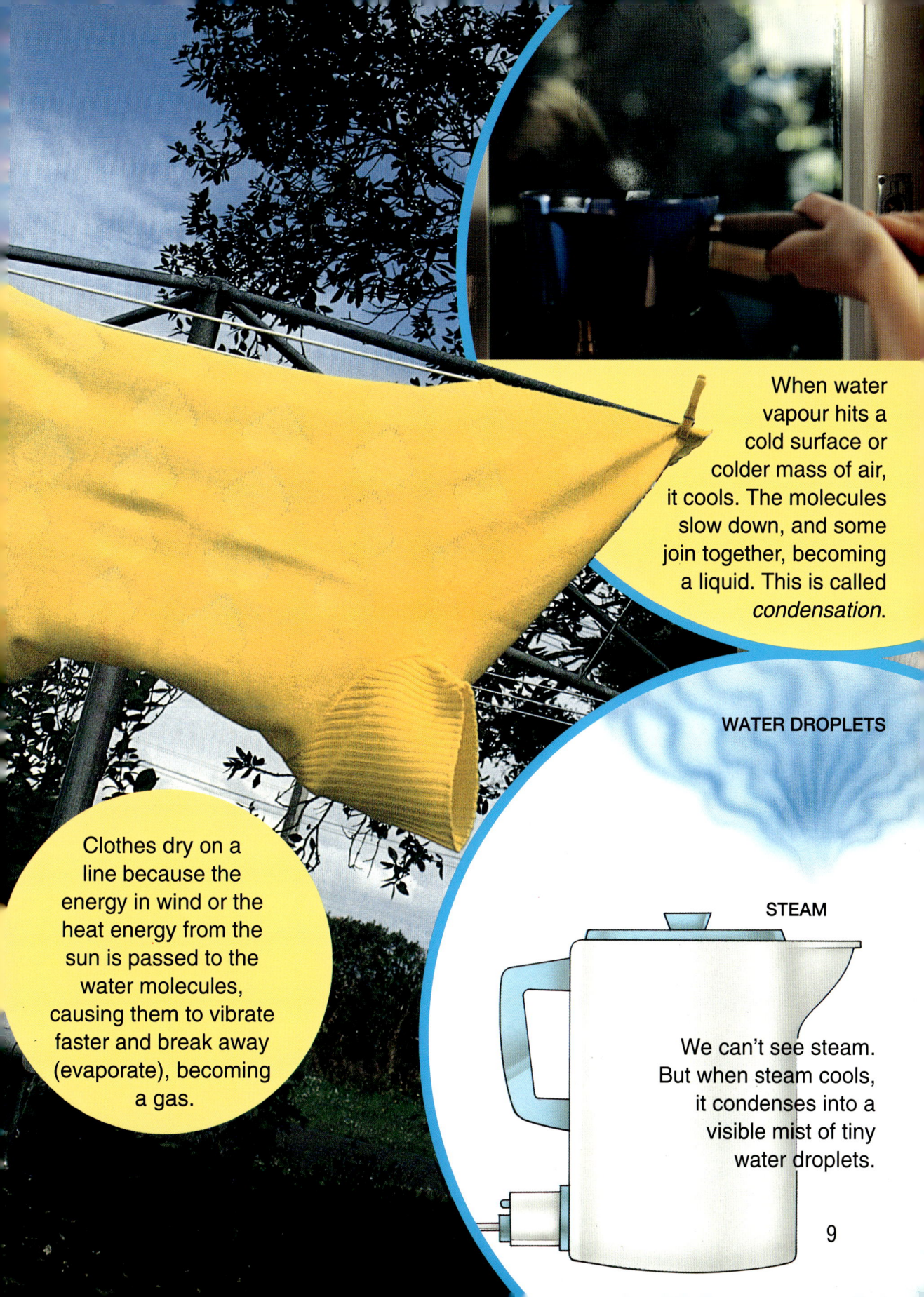

When water vapour hits a cold surface or colder mass of air, it cools. The molecules slow down, and some join together, becoming a liquid. This is called *condensation*.

WATER DROPLETS

Clothes dry on a line because the energy in wind or the heat energy from the sun is passed to the water molecules, causing them to vibrate faster and break away (evaporate), becoming a gas.

STEAM

We can't see steam. But when steam cools, it condenses into a visible mist of tiny water droplets.

9

WATER AS A SOLID

Ice is solid water. When the temperature of water falls to 0°C or below, the molecules join up to form a solid block of ice, which is very strong. Layers of ice on a pond thicker than 10 cm can easily support the weight of skaters.

Snowflakes are also solid water. When the water droplets that make up clouds freeze, they form tiny ice crystals that join together to make snowflakes. Frost occurs when water vapour condenses on plants or window-panes and then freezes into ice crystals.

Ice is a very hard substance. Many ships, including the Titanic, have sunk after hitting icebergs.

Pressure can cause the molecules in ice to break up and form a liquid. The weight of an ice-skater melts the ice under the skate's blade, making a slippery surface over which the skate can slide.

11

FLOATING & SINKING

Liquid water molecules are free to move about, and often form clusters. They are closer together than ice molecules.

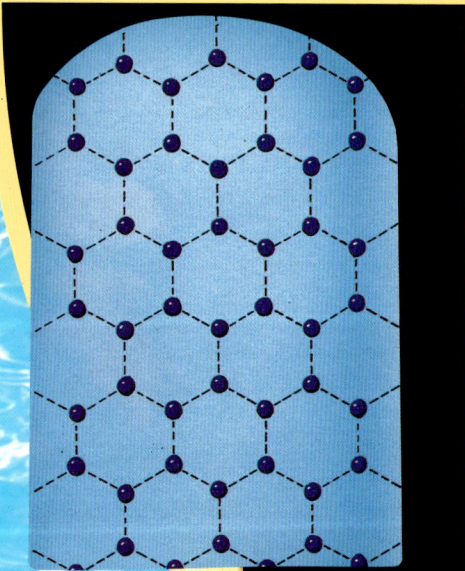

The water molecules in ice are joined together in a rigid hexagonal arrangement.

Unlike most substances, ice expands when it freezes. There is more space between the molecules in ice than between those in liquid water. As a result, ice is less *dense* than water. About one-tenth of an ice block floats above water level. Therefore, ice is about one-tenth less dense than water.

Any object will float if it, too, is less dense than water. A solid piece of balsa is less dense than water, and will float, while a solid nugget of steel is more dense, and will sink. When substances such as salt or sugar are dissolved in water, the resulting solution is more dense than pure water. People find it easier to float in salt water than fresh water.

Large quantities of salt dissolved in the water of the Great Salt Lake, in Utah, U.S.A., make floating easy. (Algae have coloured the water red.)

If ice didn't float, it would sink to the bottom of lakes and oceans, where heat energy from the sun would be unable to reach it and melt it. The ice would then destroy any life on the ocean floor.

Rivers are sometimes used to transport logs.

WATER HEATS & WATER COOLS

The water in oceans and lakes acts as a temperature regulator, preventing the earth from getting too hot or too cold to support life. Because water must absorb more of the sun's heat energy than most substances before its temperature rises, it is slow to warm. It is also slow to cool, because it releases its stored heat energy slowly.

In the process of evaporation, the warmest molecules (or those with the highest energy) are the first to break away. The remaining liquid has a cooler overall temperature. When people perspire, the warmest molecules of water on their bodies evaporate, leaving the colder (lower-energy) ones to cool them down.

Land in the middle of continents is far away from the moderating affects of the oceans. Therefore, it has greater extremes of temperature than coastal areas.

Hot water can cause serious burns because of the heat energy it contains.

Detergent and soap molecules are attracted to both water and oil. They, therefore, make excellent cleansers.

ATTRACTION & REPULSION

The attractive forces holding water molecules together are strong enough to allow the surface of water to support the weight of a small insect. These forces are also the reason why drops of water tend to be spherical, the shape that allows the molecules to be as close as possible.

Water molecules are attracted to many other things besides themselves. This is what allows water to wet things. It spreads over many surfaces and weakly binds to them. In small spaces, the attraction is stronger than the force of gravity, allowing water to move upward. We can see this happening when we dip a piece of absorbent paper in water.

Plastic and rubber are among the few things to which water is not attracted.

WATER DROP ON A PLANT

THE WATER CYCLE

The earth's water cannot be used up, as it is constantly being recycled. Even the water used by people, animals, and plants eventually returns to the water cycle.

Water is constantly evaporating from lakes and oceans, then cooling to form clouds. When the water droplets are large enough, they fall as rain or snow. Most of this moisture falls over oceans. The water that falls on land usually returns to the oceans, either by running into lakes and rivers, or by seeping into the groundwater. Even the waste water discarded by people returns to the sea via water treatment plants. Some of the water that falls on land also evaporates again, or is used by plants and animals.

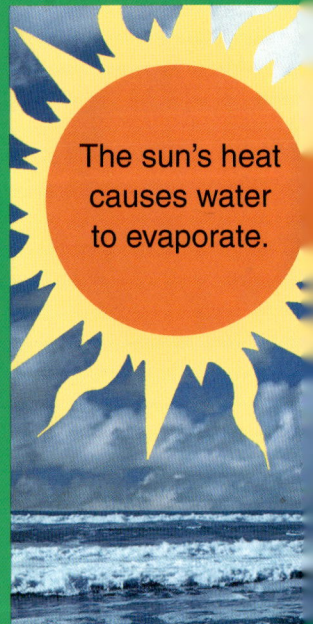

After a swim on a hot day, water on skin and hair evaporates into the air. The water will eventually fall to earth again as rain or snow. This is also what happens to water that evaporates from the oceans.

The sun's heat causes water to evaporate.

Some rain and melted snow sink into the ground, collecting in a water-saturated layer of rock. At places where this layer is level with the earth's surface, the water bubbles out to form a spring.

Water vapour condenses to liquid water as it hits a cold surface, such as food straight out of the refrigerator. We see the condensation as small drops of water.

Water vapour condenses to fall as rain, ice, or snow.

EVERY MOLECULE OF WATER PLAYS ITS PART IN THE WATER CYCLE

Water rises as invisible vapour.

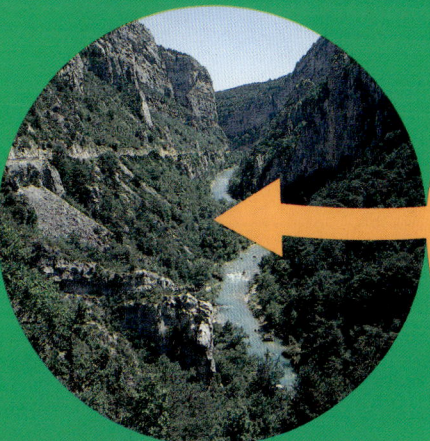

Rain and melted snow and ice trickle into streams, which in turn, link up to form rivers. Gravity causes the rivers to flow downhill until they reach a lake or ocean.

WATER & LIFE

O n its way around the water cycle, some water temporarily becomes part of plants and animals. Between 70 and 90 per cent of all living matter is water. People are two-thirds water, and fruits such as oranges and apples are three-quarters water. Blood and sap are water-based fluids. In fact, living beings are completely dependent on water. A human can survive about a month without food, but less than a week without water.

Foods that have had all their water removed are called *dehydrated* foods. They become much lighter and can be stored for longer periods. When they are soaked in water, they absorb the liquid and swell up to their original size and shape.

Jellyfish 95%
Frog 78%
Elephant 70
Dog 67%
Person 65
Weevil 48

Watermelon 97
Tomato 93%
Lemon 80%
Potato 80%
Bread 35%
Baked Sunflower
Seed 5%

Drinking too little water causes us to become dehydrated. This can cause headaches and other illnesses.

Many foods may be eaten either fresh or dried. Raisins, for instance, are grapes that have been dried in the sun.

WATER & PEOPLE

For thousands of years, people have used water for drinking, cooking, and cleaning. Although human societies are becoming more and more technology-based, people are still as reliant on water as ever before. For instance, hundreds of tons of water are needed to make every ton of steel used in a single car; ten litres of water are needed to refine one litre of petrol; and water also keeps the car's engine cool.

Although water will never run out, it can become too polluted to use. Its unique properties make it more important than oil and more precious than gold.

Without large supplies of water, many fires would rage uncontrolled.

Water theme parks use water for leisure.

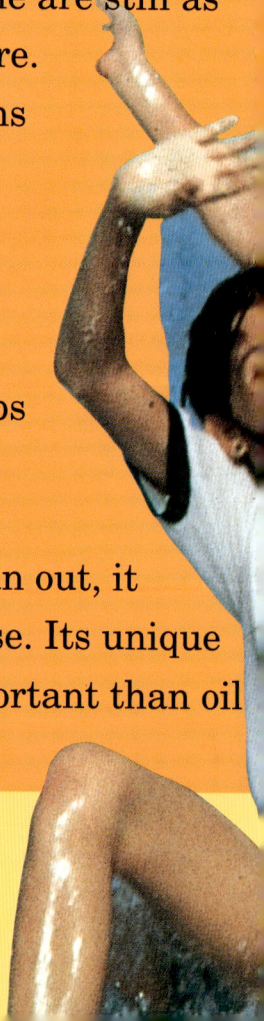

Large cities use vast amounts of water every day.

Pure drinking-water has become a product that can be bought and sold.

GLOSSARY

condensation – the process of, or the result of, a gas cooling to
become a liquid

dehydration – the removal or loss of water from a substance, such
as a plant or animal

density – the mass, or number of particles (atoms or molecules), of
a substance in a given space

dissolve – to add a substance to a liquid so that its molecules
separate from one another and mix with the liquid's molecules

evaporation – the process of a liquid becoming a gas without first
reaching its boiling point

gas – the state of matter in which the particles of a substance are
separate from one another, and expand to take up the shape
and volume of their container

liquid – the state of matter in which the particles of a substance
take up a defined amount of space (or volume), but move about
within that space. A liquid takes the shape of its container.

molecule – the smallest amount of a chemical compound that can
exist and still have the characteristics of that particular
compound. One molecule is usually made up of several atoms.

solid – the state of matter in which the particles of a substance
take up a defined amount of space and are joined together in a
rigid ordered way. The particles are not able to move about.

steam – the gaseous state of water after it reaches boiling point,
and before it expands to take up all the available space

water vapour – the gaseous state of water